ACTS OF FAITH 1

Dramas for
God's People

Advent to Easter

BRAD KINDALL

ACTS OF FAITH 1
Dramas for God's People
Advent to Easter

Contributing editor: Catherine Malotky

Editors: Scott Tunseth, James Satter

Cover and text design: James Satter

ISBN 0-8066-4493-1

The paper used in this publication meets the minimum requirements of American National Standard for Information Sciences—Permanence of Paper for Printed Library Materials, ANSI Z329.48-1984.

Manufactured in the U.S.A.

06   05   04   03   02   1   2   3   4   5   6   7   8   9   10

Contents

Foreword

The Power of Drama

Seeing is believing . . . Seeing is experiencing . . . Seeing is remembering. Stories have the power to help us believe, experience, and remember because stories help us "see." That's why Jesus spoke in parables. Because stories help us see with our hearts the kindness of God.

Drama is form of storytelling. Like the parables of Jesus, dramas help us see, experience, and remember the message. As Brad Kindall, the principal author of the dramas in this collection, says, the question in designing worship is not, "How do we say it?" but rather "How do we help them see it?" Dramas have the power to convey truth because they:

- *Visualize* the message—they help us "see" the message lived out, acted out, and put into a real context.

- *Imagine* the message—rather than hitting us between the eyes, the drama message comes to us subtly, it sneaks up on us from the side rather than from the front, drawing us in by capturing our imaginations and surprising us with truth.

Dramas move the message of the worship and sermon experience to the heart. The dramas in this collection come out of the worship experience of Community Church of Joy. Each drama was developed out of a team planning process that looks at the entire service as the message and then creates the storyline of that message using music, the sermon, video clips, dance occasion, and drama.

In some cases, the drama serves to set up the question with which the sermon will be dealing. In other cases the drama is self contained, setting up the situation and bringing it to conclusion to reinforce the point of the service and sermon. In all cases, the drama helps people see, experience, and remember the message of the service.

Though created for the worship experience, these dramas can also be used at retreats, in seminars, at banquets, and at other church events. We hope you enjoy these dramas and find them useful in your setting as you seek to help people believe, experience, and remember the kindness of God as seen in Jesus.

TIM WRIGHT
Executive Pastor and Performing Arts Coach
Community Church of Joy
Glendale, Arizona

Introduction

Using drama in the church has a long tradition in human history. For the ancient Greeks, it could even be said that drama *was* church. The great Greek dramatists were the theologians of their day, exploring their gods' interaction with human beings and the nature of life as a human community. Medieval Christian churches used dramas regularly to declare the stories of the Bible and to explore the issues behind them. Because very few people couldn't read at that time, drama was a common way to teach.

Today, when film, video games, computers, and TV have so much influenced on our lives, drama remains a powerful way to invite people to think in new ways. Drama is storytelling. It can be more engaging than a more static expository reading or telling because it taps into our emotions, making it more memorable.

The good news is that it doesn't take too much to do it well enough. For several practical suggestions, see the section "Beginning comments for the director" on page 8.

Use these dramas any time (including retreats and Bible studies), but be sure to try them in worship. Generally, they will be linked closely to preaching. They are responses to Scripture. Sometimes they are the antithesis of the themes and messages of the text.

Sometimes they are a way of looking at the themes of the text in a setting different than the biblical one— one more familiar to audiences today. In some cases, you could think of them as a choir anthem, building off the biblical text.

Using this book

This volume is one of two. The dramas in this book are related to the themes of worship for festivals and for Sundays from Advent to Pentecost. The second volume includes dramas for Sundays in the season of Pentecost. The Revised Common Lectionary, in use by many denominations, is the lectionary around which these volumes are organized.

The dramas are listed in the table of contents according the festival or Sunday of the church year to which each drama best belongs. However, there are indexes in the back of the book that organize by Bible text and by key idea. Of course, you can use these dramas wherever they fit best for you and your setting.

Each drama includes a list of characters and suggests a setting and props needed. Each drama is followed by the Prayer of the Day: This prayer generally sets the tone of the day, capturing the themes of the readings. It is included to assist worship planners as they try to create a cohesive, meaningful worship event. Please do not feel bound to use the Prayer of the Day that is listed. There are sources for new prayers (such as *Sundays*

and Seasons, published annually by Augsburg Fortress)
that may use language that feels less "churchy."

Beginning comments for the new director

None of these dramas is very complicated to stage,
but here are some things for you to remember:

- The worship service should be about the Word and
  Sacraments, not about the drama. Because of this, you
  will want to move into and out of the drama quickly,
  with a minimum of fuss. Practice, if you have props
  or a setting that needs to be set before and struck
  after. Move the stuff in and out quickly, quietly, and
  with intention.

- The people you ask to participate in the dramas
  should have clear voices, expressive faces, and a comfortable public manner. They will need to practice
  these dramas ahead of time so they can concentrate
  on what their characters are saying and doing rather
  than on what comes next and where they are supposed to be standing. They don't have to memorize
  their lines, but they need to know them well enough
  to be able to make eye contact with each other and
  the audience when needed.

- Feel free to cast the characters across gender and age
  lines when appropriate. In most cases, a woman can
  play a man's part or visa versa with a couple of slight

changes in the lines of those who refer to him or her. You might even experiment with casting a child or a woman as God's voice, to help people stretch and keep things less predictable. When names are used in the dramas, use names that reflect the breadth of ethnicities in your community.

- Keep it simple. Because you will be in a space that is used for other purposes, it may have steps and other hazards for the actors, and because the dramas are short, simple is the best. Keep costuming, set, and stage movement to a minimum.

- Try to arrange for good lighting. Most church sanctuaries were not built for excellent illumination for the area where you will most likely be performing. If possible, try to buy or rent a few stage lights. Hang them 45 degrees to the actors. That angle creates the fewest strange shadows of faces, which makes it easier to understand what they actors are saying (because you can see their faces better).

- If you can also have the ability to dim the lights, that would add enormously to your ability to set a mood. A spotlight can be okay, but it would be more helpful to invest in better general lighting that you can control and adjust.

- Use your PA system if it is any good at all. If you have wireless microphones for the actors, that is the best, but there may not be enough of them to go around.

If your system is not very flexible, you may want to rely on a reader's theater style of staging rather than asking actors to pass microphones around. Set the actors up with music stands arranged around a few standing microphones. Identify someone to explain the setting at the beginning. Some of the dramas lend themselves to this nicely. With some, this style won't be as interesting, but it will be much better than having the primary energy of the drama be about getting the microphone to the person who is going to speak next!

Just like anything we do in worship, the point is to glorify God and to help people come to new understandings about their relationship with God. The dramas are a cog in the worship wheel, no more important than other parts of the worship service. For a while, dramas will seem special (and some people may even see them as offensive or not worshipful). But if you do them enough, worshipers will come to see them as just another way of exploring what God is doing with us in this worship service.

Help! We Want to Start a Drama Ministry!

*A drama about creating Sunday
morning worship dramas*

Key idea: Creating, casting, rehearsing and performing
successful worship dramas.

Characters: Pastor Bob
Diane (a new drama director)
Brad Kindall (the writer of this collection
of sketches)

Setting: a coffee house

Props: a table, chairs, cup of coffee for each character

Bob: Brad, thanks for taking time to chat with us.

Brad: It's my pleasure, Pastor Bob. I can't resist free
coffee!

Bob: I'd like you to meet our new drama director,
Diane. Diane, this is Brad.

Brad: It's a pleasure to meet an eager volunteer.

Diane: I don't know if I'm eager yet.

Bob: Diane's an answer to prayer. She has a great heart.

Diane: And very little experience.

Brad: That'll often work in your favor. Don't worry.

Bob: Brad, as you know, we want to start doing weekly skits in our worship services.

Brad: Call them sketches, please. The word *skits* reminds me of junior-high.

Bob: Okay, *sketches*. We want to do Sunday morning dramatic sketches, so I conned . . . I mean *encouraged* . . . Diane to spearhead this vital new evangelistic tool.

Diane: *(whispering to Brad)* He promised me I'd get a hot tub in my heavenly mansion if I said yes.

Brad: *(whispering back)* He pulled that one on me, too.

Bob: Now, Brad, what kind of budget do you think we'll need? I'm thinking of asking the board for ten-thousand dollars.

Brad: *(choking on his coffee)* Bob, you're producing five-minute Sunday morning dramas—not *Les Miserable*. You'll need some money to buy scripts and props, but that's about all.

Bob: What about the fog machine? What about the spotlights and the laser show?

Brad: Fluff. You want your dramas to represent what you're congregation is going through on a weekly basis. All that stuff would just get in the way.

Diane: So what kind of props do we need?

Brad: A couch, a table, and chairs. Those few things will last you quite a while.

Bob: What about the robes and fake beards? You know, the biblical garb.

Brad: If you're going to minister to shepherds and wise men, then by all means go buy a bunch of bathrobes and sandals. If you're going to minister to people who look like you and me, let your actors dress like you and me. You want your congregation to identify with the scenes you produce.

Diane: Are you trying to tell me I don't have to make costumes?

Brad: Making costumes is very low on my priority list. If you make a costume for every Sunday, you'll burn out in a month. The key to making your drama ministry successful is to keep it simple.

Bob: Okay, I understand. We need to keep it simple.

Brad: Sure. Now, let's talk about picking scripts.

Bob: I like the funny ones.

Brad: Yes, funny is good. But the determining factor should be whatever the theme is for the day. I like to think of a worship service as a finished jigsaw puzzle. Separately, the pieces don't make a lot of sense. But together they communicate a finished product. The music, the biblical text, the drama, and sermon should all work together to communicate effectively.

Diane: So, how do I know what the pastor going to preach on?

Brad: I recommend that the two of you sit down with your worship planning team about six weeks in advance to piece together every aspect of the worship service.

Bob: Now, what if you we're the worship planning team? There's just the two of us.

Brad: That's a fine beginning, but work toward having a team of people. The worship leader, pastor, drama director, technical director, and even some lay people will all contribute to a more creative worship experience. A room of creative minds will help keep your worship services from being predictable.

Diane: Isn't church supposed to be predictable?

Bob: Of course not!

Diane: *(turning to Pastor Bob)* But our services are always the same.

Bob: That's why we're adding drama!

Diane: Where should the dramas go in the service?

Bob: How about before the message?

Diane: That sounds a little . . . predictable.

Brad: I like them before the message, too, but sometimes they might go better in the middle of the message, or after the message. The placement of every aspect of your service should not be "what we did last week," but what best serves the service and what you are trying to communicate.

Diane: What about actors? I played a spear-carrier in my high school's production of *Romeo and Juliet*. But other than me, there aren't any experienced actors.

Brad: I've found that experience is wonderful but not necessary. Some of the worst actors I know are the ones with the most experience. The "diamond in the rough" is the lay person who is comfortable on stage and acts as if they are a real person. The big voice and the broad gestures really just get in the way.

Bob: So, how do we find these people?

Brad: I'd recommend you find a script that will accompany the sermon well, and then find people in your congregation who remind you of the people in the script. Get them in a rehearsal and simply ask them to be themselves except louder.

Diane: That brings up a good point. How much should we rehearse?

Brad: As much as possible. I would recommend a rehearsal one to two weeks before the performance, then another rehearsal a couple of days before the performance, and then one the morning of the performance. If it's a highly technical piece, make sure you add the technical elements well before the Sunday morning performance.

Diane: What do you mean by *technical*?

Brad: Lights, sound, props, and so on.

Diane: We have one microphone behind the pulpit, fluorescent lights, and Ed the sound guy.

Bob: Ed comes five minutes before the service, turns my mic up to 7 and then reads a magazine for the rest of the service.

Brad: How many people does your sanctuary seat?

Bob: About 150.

Brad: You probably won't need to worry about sound amplification. Just make sure you work with your actors and encourage them to project. As long as the sketches communicate effectively, your congregation will be very forgiving of your lack of technical prowess.

Diane: I'm worried we won't have enough room on our stage.

Brad: Yeah, I once served a church with a huge pulpit that was impossible to move and a grand piano on stage. You simply have to work around those things. You can even use them. That's something that a lot of drama directors forget. Use your surroundings to your advantage.

Bob: Well, Brad, thanks for your two cents. Anything else we need to know?

Brad: Yes. Strive for excellence, but don't beat yourself up for mistakes and mishaps. This will be a growing process. You will learn something new every week. You'll get better and better. That's half the fun. Also, be prepared for people to start expecting dramas in your service. We are ministering in a highly visual culture. People like to know it's okay to have fun in church, too. I've found that people tend to lean forward in their seats when it comes time for the drama in our services. They never know what's going to happen, so it peaks their interest.

Diane: A church service where you don't know what's going to happen next? I didn't know such a thing existed. I think I might be eager now!

Brad: Great. I'm betting you're going to have a blast.

Bob: Anything else, Brad?

Brad: Can I get more coffee?

God's Walking Gift

Text: Matthew 1:18-25 (v. 23)

Key idea: "God with us" means that God knows and loves us.

Characters: Dave
                    Jesus (offstage voice)

Setting: Dave's living room

Props: box, wrapping paper, tape, scissors, stapler

Dave: *(offstage)* I don't know, honey! Put in a video for them. I have one more gift to wrap. I just need five minutes!

(Dave enters and angrily and poorly wraps package first with cellophane tape and finally with a staple gun.)

Dave: Jesus, I can't take it anymore! What in the world were you thinking with this holiday? This time of year is . . . Ah, the stress. There's just too much! If you had any idea what it was like, you never would have . . .

Jesus: Excuse me.

Dave: I said, if you had any idea what it was like down here you would have . . .

Jesus: I know exactly what you're talking about.

Dave: Okay, yeah, I know you're God and everything, but you have no idea what it's like to cart three kids around the mall the Saturday before Christmas.

Jesus: Oh, really? Well, why don't you try carting twelve disciples and a bunch of other followers around the streets of Jerusalem during Passover?

Dave: Huh?

Jesus: Wall-to-wall people—and no deodorant back then.

Dave: What are you trying to say?

Jesus: I'm trying to tell you that I know what you *have* gone through. I know what you *are* going through, and I know what you *will* go through. The circumstances may be different, but the feelings are the same.

Dave: Oh, come on! You never had kids!

Jesus: What are you talking about? What are you? You're one of my kids! I have billions of children. And they all cry and whine and make me want to pull out my spiritual hair sometimes, but I still love them.

Dave: Wow! I've always kind of thought of you as . . . I don't know . . . more spiritual.

Jesus: Hey, if you want to worship a Jesus who never went through the kind of stuff you go through, that's your option, . . . but it's not the truth. That book I wrote explains that I was fully human and fully God.

Dave: You wrote a book? I want to get it. What's it called?

Jesus: I'll spell it for you: B-I-B-L-E.

Dave: "Bee-bluh"?

Jesus: Bible.

Dave: Oh, yeah, I keep forgetting you wrote that.

Jesus: Tell me something. Who wrote *The 7 Habits of Highly Effective People* ?

Dave: Stephen R. Covey.

Jesus: How do you know?

Dave: I read that book.

Jesus: My point exactly. See what I'm getting at?

Dave: Yeah, yeah, yeah, I get it.

Jesus: Anyway, my bestseller will tell you everything you need to know about my humanity and my divinity.

Dave: *(pause)* So you went to the bathroom and everything?

Jesus: *(sarcastically)* No, the angels did it for me. . . . Of course I went to the bathroom!

Dave: Wow! Did you ever get so mad you wanted to throw something?

Jesus: Read the Gospel of John, chapter 2. I tossed a bunch of money-changers out of the temple.

Dave: Oh yeah, I remember that story. You were ticked. Hey, did you ever get so stressed out you just wanted to throw in the towel?

Jesus: In the Garden of Gethsemane, just before my arrest, I was pretty worried about having to die a very painful death.

Dave: Oh, of course. I'm sorry. I forgot about that story. *(Trying to find a way to sound empathetic)* That must have been a very tough time.

Jesus: You have no idea.

Dave: Why'd you do it? I mean, you're God. You didn't have to.

Jesus: Dave, imagine this. Imagine your children have no idea who you are or how much you love them. And imagine that they're lost and lonely and can't find their way home. What would you do?

Dave: I'd go out and try to find them.

Jesus: What if it meant losing your life to save theirs? Would you still do it?

Dave: Yeah, I guess so.

Jesus: Well, for me there was no "I guess so" about it. I love my children, and I would do it again if I had to.

Dave: Really?

Jesus: Really.

Dave: *(pause)* Thank you.

Jesus: Merry Christmas.

Stir up your power, O Lord, and come.
Take away the hindrance of our sins and make us
ready for the celebration of your birth, that we may
receive you in joy and serve you always. For you
live and reign with the Father and the Holy Spirit,
now and forever. Amen

The Shepherd

Text: Luke 1:39-55 (vv. 46-55)

Key idea: Jesus' birth did not bring complete safety to the world.

Character: Shepherd
(This drama is a monologue.)

Setting: a field

Props: a shepherd's staff

Shepherd: *(Yelling to the sheep in the distance)* Hey, come on you guys! No fighting. There's plenty of grass to go around. Come on, Lambchop, share with your sister.

(Startled by the audience's presence) Ah! Don't ever sneak up on a shepherd like that! You could have spooked the whole flock.

What?

Oh, yeah, I saw Jesus. Just last week. You with the press?

Good. I had *The National Enquirer* out here yesterday. They kept wanting me to say the angels were aliens.

Yeah, I said angels.

You didn't hear about the *angels*?

Wow. Maybe I had better start from the beginning. Me and my pals we were over . . . You see that hillside? We were hangin' with the sheep over there. It was getting pretty late. I was tired. Suddenly this guy, this angel, comes up and says, "Fear not!" I'm like, "Yeah, right." I'm telling you I have never been sore afraid in my entire life.

Anyway, this angel says, "I got good news! Tonight in Bethlehem the Messiah is being born."

I'm like, "No way!"

And the angel looks at me real serious, as if to say, "No way!" And then this whole chorus of angels fills the sky and starts to sing, "Glory to God in the highest! Peace on earth, Good will toward men." It was a kickin' song. Even the sheep were dancing!

So me and my friends say, "Let's go check this out." So we did, and we found the baby and the mom and dad in Bethlehem, staying in this stinky stable. And there was this kid there playing this drum. *Prum-pum-pum-pum. Prum-pum-pum-pum.* Over and over again. And the mom and dad were being really polite and smiling and nodding, but I could tell they were like "enough with the drum already!" So I told the kid to quit it with the drum and he turns to me and says, "This is the only gift I have." And I said, "That's all well and good, but you keep waking up the baby!" So he quit for a while. And that's pretty much how it happened.

Huh? The other shepherds? Oh, they all went to tell all of their friends about the baby and the angels and everything. Well, I was going to go with them, but then I got to thinking, "Is this really practical?" I mean, how do we know the baby is really the one?

Yeah, I know the angels said he was, but how do we know we can trust the angels? How do we know the angels were really even there?

I know, I know. Yeah, we all saw them, but it was dark and we were really tired.

Hey, listen, the bottom line is that I got a job to do. I'm a shepherd. I watch sheep. If I leave these sheep, I could lose my job. Besides, I have a feeling most people wouldn't believe me if told them what I just told you. The safe thing to do is stay here and keep it to myself. If you were me, wouldn't you do the same?

Uh-oh, where are my sheep? Oh, there they are. I'd better go get them.

(While exiting) Hey, come on you guys, get out of the lake. You just ate. You're going to get cramps and drown. Crazy sheep!

Stir up your power, O Lord, and come. Take away the hindrance of our sins and make us ready for the celebration of your birth, that we may receive you in joy and serve you always. For you live and reign with God and the Holy Spirit, now and forever. Amen

Crisscrossed Christmas

Text: Titus 3:4-7

Key idea: Christmas traditions go many directions. Only one is toward Christ.

Characters: Leslee
                Bill
                Julie *(Leslee and Bill's daughter)*
                Tommy *(Leslee and Bill's son)*

Setting: Bill and Leslee's living room. Bill reads the newspaper and Leslee drinks a cup of coffee.

Props: furniture, newspaper, cup of coffee

Leslee: Honey?

Bill: Yes.

Leslee: I've been thinking.

Bill: Uh-oh.

Leslee: Well, it's Christmas Eve and I'm worried that the kids don't understand what Christmas is really all about.

Bill: Uh-huh.

Leslee: I asked Tommy the other day what the meaning of Christmas was to him and he said, "To score major payload."

Bill: That's my boy!

Leslee: That's pathetic! I went shopping the other day with Julie and she told me she thinks Christmas was invented by St. François Gerbaud.

Bill: Who's that?

Leslee: He's a fashion designer!

Bill: Leslee, you're overreacting.

Leslee: We are responsible for these young lives, Bill! Now, I'm going to call them in here, and I want you to tell them the Christmas story.

(Leslee walks to the edge of the stage.)

Bill: Why do I have to do it?

Leslee: Julie! Tommy! Would you come in here for a minute?

Julie and Tommy: *(offstage)* No!

Leslee: You kids get in here this instant!

(Tommy and Julie enter, groaning.)

Leslee: Kids, your dad would like to tell you the Christmas story.

Tommy: Couldn't we rent the movie?

Leslee: No.

Julie: Is this going to take long? I'm expecting a call.

Leslee: That can wait. Go ahead, Bill.

Bill: *(pause)* Couldn't we rent the movie?

Leslee: No, now get to it!

Bill: Right. Kids, Rudolph the red-nosed reindeer, had a very shiny nose.

Leslee: Honey!

Bill: And if you ever saw it, you would even say it . . .

Leslee: Bill, that's the wrong story.

Bill: It is? Well, which one were you thinking of?

Leslee: The one about Jesus!

Bill: Oh! Right! Okay, let's see. God, had a Son, and that boy . . .

Tommy: Do we believe in God?

Bill: Honey?

Leslee: Yes!

Bill: Yes! Okay, now, God gave his Son to a young couple named Mary and Joseph.

Tommy: Were there dinosaurs back then?

Bill: Honey?

Leslee: No!

Bill: No.

Tommy: Shoot! I think this story is going to need some dinosaurs.

Bill: Okay, Mary and Joseph went to a little village called . . .

Leslee: Bethlehem.

Bill: Right. Bethlehem. And they tried to get a hotel but there wasn't any room, so they had to go out and have the baby in a stable.

Julie: Stop right there! If God's all-powerful and everything, don't you think God could have called ahead to get a reservation?

Bill: Are you getting smart with me?

Julie: It's a logical question, Dad.

Bill: No it's not. Just think about all the nativity scenes all over the world. They're cute as a button. Take that away and put Jesus in the Bethlehem Hilton, and you ruin the whole nativity-scene industry. I don't think God would do that!

Leslee: Bill, go on.

Bill: Where was I? Okay, now there were shepherds out in the field keeping watch over their flocks by night.

Tommy: And T-rex came and ate them!

Bill: Thanks, Tommy. That'll be enough.

Tommy: I was just trying to help.

Bill: And an angel appeared to the shepherds and told them about the birth of the baby Jesus. And the shepherds were kinda' shaking in their boots, but the angel told them to relax. And then a bunch of angels appeared in the sky and sang.

Tommy: What did they sing?

Bill: Honey?

Leslee: *Gloria in excelsis deo.*

Tommy: Sing it.

Leslee: I don't know how it goes.

Tommy: You sing it, Dad.

Bill: *(singing Van Morrison's "Gloria" from the 1993* Too Long in Exile *album)* Gloria! G-L-O-R-I-A. *Gloria in excelsis deo.*

Julie: Oh, brother.

Bill: So the shepherds went to Bethlehem to see the baby and brought him gifts, but one of the shepherds had no gift except his little drum . . .

Leslee: Bill . . .

Bill: But then the little drummer boy realized that he could play the drum and that would be his gift. He was so proud as he played: *Prum-pum-pum-pum. Prum-pum-pum-pum.*

Leslee: Bill! The drummer boy was added later for the song.

Bill: I don't think so.

Leslee: I *do* think so. Go on!

Bill: Anyway, today we celebrate Christmas to celebrate God's Son, Jesus, coming to earth as a baby.

Tommy: What happened to Jesus after he grew up?

Bill: *(To Leslee)* Hon?

Leslee: Well, he healed a lot of people and taught people about God.

Julie: And then they killed him.

Bill: Leave it to Julie to put a positive spin on everything.

Julie: Well, that's how the story goes, Dad.

Tommy: Why did they kill him?

Leslee: Because . . . Bill?

Bill: Because . . . he was so nice to everyone?

Julie: Guess it doesn't pay to be nice, eh, Dad?

Bill: Well . . .

Tommy: This doesn't make sense. Why would God let them do that to Jesus?

Leslee: Well, honey, Jesus is God.

Tommy: But God shouldn't have let that happen!

Leslee: I think he did it because he loves us.

Julie: That's not love. That's stupidity.

Bill: You watch your mouth.

Julie: Admit it! Why on earth would the Almighty God be caught dead here? If God knows all and sees all, God would know better!

Bill: *(pause)* Hon, I don't think this is going well.

(Leslee is silenced by the dilemma.)

Tommy: Tell the other story, Dad.

Julie: *(Shaking her head)* I'm outta here. *(She exits.)*

Bill: Okay. Rudolph, the red-nosed-reindeer, had a very shiny nose. And if you ever saw it, you would even say it glows.

Almighty God, you have made yourself known in your Son, Jesus Christ, redeemer of the world. We pray that his birth as a human child will set us free from the slavery of our sin. Through Jesus Christ our Lord, who lives and reigns with you and the Holy Spirit, one God, now and forever. Amen

Walter the Whiner

Text: Colossians 3:12-17

Key idea: Integrating Christianity into the fabric of life.

Characters: Walter
Dr. Gonzalez

Setting: a psychologist's office

Props: two chairs, other office furniture

(Dr. Gonzalez brightens up as Walter enters.)

Gonzalez: Hello, Walter, I'm so glad to meet you. I'm Dr. Gonzalez. Please have a seat. Would you like some coffee?

Walter: I get a sour stomach.

Gonzalez: Would you like some water?

Walter: Is it bottled?

Gonzalez: No, I'm sorry.

Walter: I'll survive.

Gonzalez: Well, Walter, what's on your mind today?

Walter: Nobody likes me.

Gonzalez: I see. What gives you that impression?

Walter: No one's ever liked me. When I was growing up, all the kids at school called me "Walter the whiner."

Gonzalez: That must have really hurt you.

Walter: The world is a cold, dark place, Doctor.

Gonzalez: What makes you say that?

Walter: Wake up and smell the coffee! Evil is all around us. We got your global warming. And I have a sour stomach!

Gonzalez: Walter, let's talk about your friends.

Walter: I don't have any friends.

Gonzalez: Why do you suppose that is?

Walter: People are mean! Everybody's looking out for themselves.

Gonzalez: Have you ever had any friends?

Walter: I had a cocker spaniel once.

Gonzalez: What happened to it?

Walter: She didn't like me. Every time I tried to pet her, she'd just growl. See, even the animal kingdom hates me.

Gonzalez: Walter, look at this glass of water for a second. Is it half empty or is it half full?

Walter: Who cares? It's filled with mercury, and lead and it's going to kill you!

Gonzalez: I see. Walter, let's talk about something that gives you joy.

Walter: Well, let's see. . . . I guess I'd have to say my relationship with Jesus Christ.

Gonzalez: Oh, you're a religious man?

Walter: It's not a religion! It's a relationship!

Gonzalez: I see. Tell me about the joy you find in Jesus.

Walter: Well, I guess I find joy in Jesus because I know I'll go to heaven and get off this godforsaken planet!

Gonzalez: Walter, do you think Jesus was a joy-filled person?

Walter: No, of course not. If you knew you were going to die, like he did, would you be happy?

Gonzalez: I don't know. I always thought of Jesus as a positive person.

Walter: He had no home. He had no money. And he had no friends.

Gonzalez: What about the twelve disciples?

Walter: Freeloaders, all of 'em!

Gonzalez: I see. Well, Walter, our time is up. I think we should schedule an appointment for next week. What do you think?

Walter: Couldn't we meet tomorrow? Maybe for lunch or dinner?

Gonzalez: I'm sorry I can't.

Walter: Oh, but I'd love to tell you about my life-changing encounter with Jesus Christ.

Gonzalez: If Jesus Christ is going to do to me what he's done to you, I'll stay an agnostic.

Walter: But he'll give you the peace that passes all understanding!

Gonzalez: Walter, it appears to me he's given you a sour stomach. See you next week.

Walter: If I live that long.

Gonzalez: See you later.

Walter: Only if we're lucky.

Almighty God, you have made yourself known in your Son, Jesus Christ, redeemer of the world. We pray that his birth as a human child will set us free from the slavery of our sin; through Jesus Christ our Lord, who lives and reigns with you and the Holy Spirit, one God, now and forever. Amen

Peculiar Petitions

Text: Matthew 5:5-13

Key idea: Prayer is more than a formula with easy answers.

Characters: Dr. Shaman Guru
Audience Member 1
Audience Member 2
Audience Member 3
Questioner

Setting: a self-help seminar in an auditorium

Props: slide, sign, or overhead-projection with the word *Applause* on it

Announcer: Ladies and gentlemen, please give a big round of applause for the honorable Dr. Shaman Guru.

(Slide: Applause)

Guru: *(Stands in the form of a question mark.)* What am I?

Audience Member 1: You're a flower!

Guru: No.

Audience Member 2: You're rain!

Guru: No.

Audience Member 3: You're a nut!

Guru: No, I'm a question mark. We all are question marks looking for the universal answer. Do you have a question for me? Speak and I will answer.

Questioner: Dr. Guru, I'm a big fan. Could you tell me why my prayers aren't answered?

Guru: I'm sorry, I did not hear you. What did you say?

Questioner: Could you tell me why my prayers are not answered?

Guru: Child, come forward.

(The Questioner comes forward.)

Guru: What is your name?

Questioner: I have no name. I am a question mark.

Guru: Oh, good answer. Question Mark, to whom do you pray?

Questioner: Well, I just kind of throw the words out there and hope someone picks them up.

Guru: Ahh! See, you are not being specific enough. You have to choose a god.

Questioner: That seems so narrow.

Guru: When you send a letter, you have to put an address on it, do you not?

Questioner: Yeah, I see your point.

Guru: Now, after you've picked a deity, you have to have the right form. How do you stand when you pray?

Questioner: I just kinda fold my hands like I did in Sunday school.

Guru: Ah! No! You must not fold the hands for then you will cut off one of the main chakra points.

Questioner: Chakra points?

Guru: The body has many chakra points connecting us to the oneness of the universe.

Questioner: How do *you* stand?

Guru: Like this.

(Guru stands in a ridiculous pose—hands in the air, back arched, standing on tip-toes, mouth and eyes wide open.)

Guru: See how open I am!

Questioner: I'm afraid I might hurt myself.

Guru: No, you'll be fine! Try it.

Questioner: *(Trying to make the same pose.)* How do I look?

Guru: Like a tulip.

Questioner: Is that good?

Guru: Yes, God loves flowers.

Questioner: So you think God will answer my prayers now?

Guru: Are you a good person or a bad person?

Questioner: I think I'm bad.

Guru: Let me see your eyes.

Questioner: Am I bad?

Guru: Well, you're not great.

Questioner: What should I do?

Guru: *(pause)* Recycle.

Questioner: Recycle?

Guru: You don't recycle, do you?

Questioner: *(realizing he's been found out)* It's so much work.

Guru: That's no excuse. The earth is dying, and you are killing it!

Questioner: *(almost to the point of tears)* I'm sorry!

Guru: No wonder God doesn't like you!

Questioner: I'll try to do better.

Guru: I should hope so! Recycle all your trash. Then come back in a month, and I'll bet God will answer your prayers.

Questioner: Thank you, Dr. Guru.

Guru: *(suddenly out of breath)* Oh, I'm tired. That was a tough one. I must go and take a mud bath . . . so good for the pores. Thank you, children, for coming. I love you.

Announcer: Ladies and gentlemen, please give a big round of applause for the honorable Dr. Shaman Guru.

(Slide: Applause)

＊＋═＋═＋＋

O God, you know that we cannot withstand the dangers that surround us. Strengthen us in body and spirit so that, with your help, we may be able to overcome the weakness that our sin has brought upon us; through Jesus Christ, your Son, our Lord. Amen

Common Ground

Text: 1 Corinthians 8:1-13 (vv. 1-8)

Key idea: Freedom in Christ.

Characters: Lori
                Kim
                Jack *(Lori's 8-year-old son)*

Setting: Lori's kitchen

Props: table, chairs, coffeepot, coffee mugs,
        Jack's Halloween costume

Lori: *(enters with coffeepot)* Here we go.

(Lori pours coffee for Kim.)

Kim: This is so nice of you.

Lori: I remember what it was like when we first moved in. You want to find some friends for your kids, but you don't know their parents, and it's hard to just walk up to someone's door and introduce yourself.

Kim: Yeah, and every neighborhood has their own rules about what's appropriate. Like, does the mom call and ask if it's okay for the kids to come over, or do the kids just walk over and knock on the door?

Lori: Oh, just knock on the door. We're very laid back around here.

Kim: Oh, I'm so glad.

(Lori's son Jack walks in wearing a Halloween costume.)

Jack: Trick or treat!

Lori: Well, look who's here. I think there are some suckers in the pantry. Go grab some and share them with the kids in the other room.

Kim: Cute costume.

Lori: Hey, why don't we get the kids together and go trick-or-treating together?

Kim: Oh, sorry, we don't celebrate Halloween.

Lori: *(pause)* What?

Kim: We just don't make a big deal of it.

Lori: You don't celebrate Halloween?

Kim: No. As we looked at the holiday and its origins in the occult, we felt like it was something we'd rather not have our kids involved in.

Lori: The occult? Well, we're not involved in the occult.

Kim: Oh, I'm not saying you are. Please don't misunderstand me.

Lori: I mean, Jack's only eight years old. He just likes the candy.

Kim: Oh, I'm sure . . .

Lori: We go with him around the neighborhood. There's no way he could do any animal sacrifices. We're with him all the time.

Kim: I know, but I read that Halloween is the most active night of the year for satanic practices.

Lori: Well, I don't know about that stuff. It's just a family holiday around here. *(pause)* How do you feel about Arbor Day?

Kim: All for it.

Lori: Groundhog Day?

Kim: Sure.

Lori: St. Patrick's Day?

Kim: I'll be in green.

Lori: But no Halloween?

Kim: Sorry.

Lori: Hmmm . . . So do you think I'm doing damage to my kids by letting them trick-or-treat?

Kim: All I'm saying is that it's not for us. We just don't feel it's right to glorify the dark side.

Lori: I don't think we're glorifying the dark side.

Kim: Oh, of course not.

Lori: So, what does your family do on Halloween?

Kim: We usually rent a movie. I know! Why don't you come over after you go trick-or-treating?

Lori: What is the movie rated?

Kim: PG-13.

Lori: Sorry, but we have a hard-and-fast rule the kids can only see G-rated movies. Is there something else we could do?

Kim: Well, our kids have some video games?

Lori: Do they involve guns?

Kim: Well, yeah, a couple of them do.

Lori: We don't let our kids have anything to do with guns.

Kim: Maybe we could just have a barbecue.

Lori: We're vegetarians.

Kim: How can you survive without meat?

Lori: How can you kill a defenseless animal?

Kim: *(pause)* Wow, I wonder if we have anything in common.

Lori: Yeah, it's kind of weird.

(They sigh.)

Kim: What are your thoughts on Jesus Christ?

Lori: *(hesitant)* I'm . . . crazy about him.

Kim: Well, I am, too.

Lori: Well, that's something.

Kim: Yeah, it's a big something.

(They banter as lights fade.)

*O God, you know that we cannot withstand
the dangers that surround us. Strengthen us in
body and spirit so that, with your help, we may
be able to overcome the weakness that our sin
has brought upon us. Through Jesus Christ,
your Son, our Lord. Amen*

Ladder-Climbing

Text: 1 Corinthians 3:10-11, 16-23

Key idea: Distracted from God by work, selfishness, pride, success.

Characters: Boss
                 Jeff

Setting: an office

Props: An envelope with a check in it. An envelope with a check, plane tickets, and a key in it. Three slides or overheads with the words *Year 1, Year 2,* and *Year 3* on them.

(Slide 1: Year 1)

Boss: Come in, Jeff, have a seat.

Jeff: Certainly.

Boss: *(looking over a report)* Well, Jeff, I usually don't enjoy these annual evaluations. I hate doling out criticism, but happily that's not going to be the case with you. I don't know if you know this, but you outsold every other salesperson in this company last year.

Jeff: I did?

Boss: You not only outsold everyone else, you broke the company record.

Jeff: Me?

Boss: Yes, you. I have to ask you, what have you been doing differently?

Jeff: I don't know . . . Well, I have been praying a lot more.

Boss: That's it?

Jeff: Yeah,. I made a commitment last year at church that I would turn my career over to God, and I guess God's blessed me for it.

Boss: I should say so. I've never been the religious sort, but this could make a believer out of even me. I don't suppose you could teach this to the rest of the staff?

Jeff: Well, this is not something I can do. This is God working.

Boss: Well, for the sake of this company, I hope God keeps up the good work.

Jeff: I have no doubts.

Boss: Thanks for coming in. *(As Jeff gets up to leave)* Hey, Jeff, you wouldn't mind praying for me if you have the chance?

Jeff: Consider it done.

Boss: Thanks.

(Slide 2: Year 2)

Boss: Come in, Jeff, have a seat.

Jeff: Certainly.

Boss: May I get you some coffee? A doughnut?

Jeff: No, thanks, I'm fine.

Boss: Well, how's my favorite employee?

Jeff: Great! Just great.

Boss: Jeff, as you probably know, you broke the company sales record again.

Jeff: Yes, I know.

Boss: So as a gesture of our thanks, Mr. Wainwright asked me to give you this. *(Hands Jeff an envelope.)*

Jeff: Thank you. *(Opens the envelope)* This is a check for 10,000 dollars . . .

Boss: Yes, I know. Congratulations, Jeff.

Jeff: Wow! I'm overwhelmed.

Boss: Jeff, how are you doing it? You still praying?

Jeff: Yes, but I've also been working harder. I've been reading more. I've been taking some business classes at night.

Boss: Well, whatever you're doing, keep it up.

Jeff: You can count on it. Thank you.

Boss: Thank *you*, Jeff.

(Slide 3: Year 3)

Boss: Jeff, my boy! Come in! Sit. Relax.

Jeff: *(cocky, arrogant)* I don't have a lot of time. Can we make this brief?

Boss: Yes, of course. Coffee?

Jeff: Do you have espresso?

Boss: I'll send someone out for some!

Jeff: Don't bother. I have to catch a plane in an hour.

Boss: I'll be brief. Jeff, the money you brought into this company this year has allowed us to expand in ways we never thought possible. So as a gesture of our thanks, Mr. Wainwright would like to double your salary, and he asked me to give you this.

(The boss hands Jeff another envelope.)

Jeff: *(opens the envelope)* Hmmm . . . let's see . . . a check for 20,000 dollars, plane tickets to Tahiti, and keys. What are the keys to?

Boss: A brand new car.

Jeff: That's very kind of you. Very kind. Well, I need to run. Where's the car?

Boss: Out front in your new parking space.

Jeff: Excellent. *(He begins to exit.)*

Boss: Jeff, I have to ask you, do you still attribute all your success to God?

Jeff: Who?

God of compassion, keep before us the love you have
revealed in your Son, who prayed even for his enemies.
In our words and deeds help us to be like him through
whom we pray, Jesus Christ our Lord. Amen

Weak-Kneed Wishes

Text: Mark 2:1-12

Key idea: Radical faith brings a radical response.

Character: Mark Spaulding
                    (This is a monologue.)

Setting: unspecified

Props: none

Mark: *(enters, wondering if anyone is present)* Hello?
Hello? Hey, God, it's me, Mark Spaulding. Are you
there? *(Pause)* I'm going to assume you are. Listen, I
know it's been a while since we talked, but I've been
really swamped at work. Money's been pretty tight
around our house, so I had to take on some extra
projects at work. Plus, Jamie's been playing soccer,
and Andrea's in dance, and Lori's working overtime
to try to help out. Our lives are totally out of control.
Anyway, in checking my calendar today I noticed I
had a little time, so I thought I'd check in. How's it
going? I'm going to assume things are good for you.
Things are going great for me. Wow! I really think
I've found my nitch. I'm on the fast track now, baby!
Whoom-zing!

(Trying unsuccessfully to convince God all is well) Things are clicking at home. My marriage is . . . wow! And the kids are growing, and they haven't been convicted of any crimes. Things are great. Busy, but great. So, hey, it's been great chatting with you. Uh . . . I'm going to go now. Uh . . . amen.

(Begins to walk away but stops himself.)

Uh . . . there is one more thing. It's just a small thing. I hesitate to even mention it. It's so small. I . . . I . . . I've been struggling with depression. I can't sleep at night, and I hate getting up in the morning. It's kind've been my little secret, and I figured that with you being God, you might be able to help me out of this black hole. You know . . . if you have the time. I'm sure you have bigger fish to fry, global crises and the like, but if you wouldn't mind putting me in your "in-basket," I'd greatly appreciate it. *(Pause.)*

Cuz I'm really hurting inside.

(Waits for some response.)

Or if you just want to pass on this one, I think I can probably figure this one out by myself. I'm a pretty smart guy. I can certainly go get a book on this topic. You know what? That's what I'm going to do. I'm going to go get a book on this. Forget I ever mentioned it. Like I said, other than this, things are going great. You go back to working on whatever you were working on, and I'll take care of this. Hey, it's been great chatting. Take care, now. Amen

(While exiting) I wonder what would happen if I really believed that God was God?

◄◄ ▬◄✦▮◄ ►►

Lord God, we ask you to keep your family,
the church, always faithful to you, that all who
lean on the hope of your promises may gain strength
from the power of your love. Through your Son,
Jesus Christ, our Lord. Amen

Wah! Wah! Wah!

Text: Matthew 6:25-34

Key idea: Worrying is an excuse to avoid real life.

Characters: Complainer *(male)*
Teenager
Adult
God *(offstage voice)*

Setting: unspecified

Props: none

Complainer: Help! Help me! Won't someone please lend a helping hand to a poor man down on his luck?

Teenager: What's the matter?

Complainer: I'm so bored!

Teenager: Is that all?

Complainer: No, no, it's much more than that. I don't feel like my life has any meaning. I don't feel needed by anyone.

Teenager: Hey, you're in luck! Every month our church goes down to a soup kitchen and helps to feed people who are homeless. Do you want to come?

Complainer: Well, let me check my calendar. I doubt I'd be available, though. My job keeps me so busy.

Teenager: What do you do?

Complainer: *(whining)* I'm a professional complainer.

Teenager: Well, I can't help you. Sorry. *(Exits.)*

Complainer: Don't go! Now, I'll feel so lonely. Oh, why do I always do that? I drive everyone off. I'm dirt. I'm scum. No one likes me! Help! Help me!

Adult: *(enters)* What's the matter?

Complainer: I don't know where to start.

Adult: Start from the beginning.

Complainer: Well, my marriage is falling apart. My wife says I'm too caught up in my work.

Adult: What do you do?

Complainer: I complain.

Adult: Have you thought of seeing a marriage counselor?

Complainer: Oh, they're so expensive.

Adult: Actually, I know one who works on a sliding scale.

Complainer: Is the counselor a man?

Adult: No, a woman.

Complainer: I wouldn't feel comfortable with a woman.

Adult: Well, I know of a male counselor, too.

Complainer: But what if he doesn't understand me? What if he takes sides? A bad counselor can do more harm than good. He could push my marriage over the edge. He could have an affair with my wife.

(Adult starts walking offstage shaking head.)

Complainer: *(stepping toward exiting Adult)* He could wear colors that clash. That could hurt my eyes and then I'd get a headache. It's going to cost money to get there. I could get lost. *(Pause)* Oh, he's gone! I did it again! Why do I always do that? I'm no good. No one likes me! No one cares for me. Help! Help me!

God: What seems to be the problem?

Complainer: Who are you?

God: I'm God.

Complainer: Oh, you're just what I need!

God: I know. What are you looking for?

Complainer: I want joy! I want peace and strength! I want freedom from my past! I want a deep relationship with my maker!

God: I'd love to give you those things!

Complainer: You would? What would I have to do?

God: Well, we need to spend time together talking each day. And it would help if you cracked open my book, the Bible. And you might want to get involved with your church beyond Sunday mornings.

Complainer: Oh, but I'm so busy with my work.

God: Perhaps you need to find another profession.

Complainer: You want me to quit my job?

God: Exactly.

Complainer: But I love my job!

God: That's the problem.

Almighty and everlasting God, ruler of heaven
and earth; hear our prayer and give us your
peace now and forever; through your Son,
Jesus Christ, our Lord. Amen

The Church of Dr. Shaman Guru

Text: John 20:24-29

Key idea: Must it be a physical resurrection?

Characters: Dr. Shaman Guru
Ryan
Announcer

Setting: an auditorium

Props: podium, stool

Announcer: Ladies and gentlemen, the guru's in the house. Please give a warm round of applause for the honorable Dr. Shaman Guru.

Guru: Welcome, my little flowers. Today I would like to discuss the person Jesus Christ. As you know, there has been a great deal of media attention regarding the Shaman Guru movement and our findings on the man, the sage, the revolutionary Jesus Christ. And while I sympathize with my critics, I cannot hide my head in the sand like my critics. I'm sure you all have questions, and as always, I have answers. The floor is open as is the universe. Someone speak and I will answer.

Ryan: Dr. Guru, in your book *Jesus Christ, Elvis Presley, and John Lennon,* you state that you believe in the "spiritual resurrection" of Jesus, but not the "physical resurrection." Could you clarify what you mean?

Guru: What's your name?

Ryan: Ryan.

Guru: Ryan, I'm going to call you "Rhododendron" for you remind me of a shrub that flowers. Rhododendron, the physical body is a shell for the spirit of a person. The Romans destroyed the physical shell of Jesus when they crucified him, but they did not destroy his spirit. His spirit lives on in the lives of his followers.

Ryan: So, the disciples saw his *spirit* on the first Easter, not his *physical* body?

Guru: I wouldn't even go that far. I believe they saw the memory of their leader as they gathered to mourn his death. The same thing happened in Central Park when John Lennon's followers gathered to mourn his death. There were many reported sightings of John Lennon today. The same can be said of Elvis Presley and his followers, and the same will be said of me after I die.

Ryan: But if Jesus didn't physically rise from the dead, then Christianity, the church, and Easter are all a big joke.

Guru: No, no, no! Easter's a wonderful holiday. So many treats for all the girls and boys! The women in their Easter bonnets. And they always show *The Ten Commandments* on TV. I love that Charlton Heston.

Ryan: But what's the point if Jesus didn't physically rise from the dead?

Guru: Rhododendron, you're throwing out the baby with the bath water. The church is a wonderful thing. It helps people. It brings them together on Sundays. It provides solace in times of grief. Why destroy a good thing?

Ryan: Why organize around a myth?

Guru: Myths are simply stories that illustrate a point of truth. The Jesus myth illustrates the importance of love and justice and mercy. Jesus may not have been the God, but he was a great teacher, and worthy of a place in history.

Ryan: I think I understand. *(Excited)* Hey, could we organize a church around John Lennon and play Beatles songs every Sunday?

Guru: Now that's a good idea! John Lennon was such a kind, loving man. He deserves a religion.

Ryan: While we're at it, why don't we just create the Shaman Guru Church, too?

Guru: Oh, I like the way you think. Would you like to be an elder?

Ryan: Sure!

Guru: Oh, this will be great fun. Of course, it will cost a lot of money. Would you be willing to give to a worthy endeavor such as this?

Ryan: Where do I sign?

Guru: There will be a booth in the lobby. Won't you all please give to the Shaman Guru Church? We will have so much fun. We'll meet once a month and I'll talk, and maybe we can even have a mime troupe. I love those mimes. This has been our most beneficial gathering yet. I can't wait to see you all in my church. We'll have such fun. I must go now. I love you. You love me. We are a happy family.

Announcer: Ladies and gentlemen, a big round of applause for the honorable Dr. Shaman Guru!

*Almighty God, with joy we celebrate the festival
of our Lord's resurrection. Graciously help us to show
the power of the resurrection in all that we say and do.
Through your Son, Jesus Christ our Lord, who lives
and reigns with you and the Holy Spirit,
one God, now and forever. Amen*

The Invitation

Text: Psalm 23 (vv. 5-6)

Key idea: God's invitation to the feast boosts our passion for life.

Characters: Mikey *(female)*
Secretary
God *(offstage voice)*

Scene 1

Setting: Mikey's office. She sits at a desk surrounded by paperwork, talking on the telephone.

Props: desk, phone, computer, and other office equipment

Mikey: *(on the phone)* I know. I know. I apologize for that. You are perfectly justified in saying that. And I want you to know I will do everything in my power to assure this doesn't happen again. Okay? . . . Okay. . . . Bye.

Secretary: *(enters)* Ray Costantino is on the line. He wants to know if you have the proposal done.

Mikey: Tell him I'm waiting for a quote from Graphics.

Secretary: He said he needs it by noon.

Mikey: Judy, I haven't even started his proposal. Tell him I can't move on it until I get the quote.

Secretary: Okay. Oh, and your husband is on the phone. Line two. *(Exits.)*

Mikey: What? Why can't you pick him up? . . . Well, I'm sorry. I'm in meetings all afternoon. . . . Would you lighten up? There'll be other Little League games. I'll make the next one. Anyway, he says I make him nervous when I'm there. . . . Hey, don't start with that. This job is paying for your car payment. . . . Don't start complaining now. . . . I am not in a bad mood. I just happen to work for a living. . . . What? . . . Seven o'clock. I have a job, honey. . . . Hello? Hello?

Secretary: *(enters)* Jason Reeves says you're supposed to be in a meeting with him and the Cummings group.

Mikey: Oh, shoot! Shoot! Tell him I'll be there in 15 minutes.

Secretary: And Erin Hodge just called and wants to know why you're not over at the development meeting.

Mikey: Tell her I'll be there in 15 minutes!

Secretary: It's not the same meeting, Mikey.

Mikey: Shoot! Tell her I'll be there in an hour.

Secretary: Okay. *(Exits.)*

Mikey: I'm an idiot. I gotta get my head on straight.

Secretary: *(enters)* Mikey, Erin says the meeting will be over in an hour.

Mikey: Well, tell her I just threw up all over my desk and I've come down with a case of leprosy.

Secretary: You've got to be kidding.

Mikey: I don't care what you tell her. Just get her off my back.

Secretary: I'm not going to lie for you.

Mikey: Fine. Tell her I forgot, and that I'll make it up to her later.

Secretary: Okay. Oh, and I just got an e-mail from Barbara. Cornish wants to see you in his office at eleven.

Mikey: Cornish? What does he want?

Secretary: I don't know. The memo just says it's important.

Mikey: Tell Barbara I'll be there.

Secretary: Okay. *(Exits.)*

Mikey: I'm dead. I'm sunk. Cornish never wants to see me. I wonder what I did. It must've been bad, whatever it is.

Secretary: (enters) Mikey, a gentleman just dropped this off. He said it's urgent.

Mikey: Let me see it. *(Opens the invitation and reads.)* What in the world?

Secretary: What is it?

Mikey: It's an invitation to a banquet.

Secretary: Who's the guest of honor?

Mikey: Me.

Secretary: Who's it from?

Mikey: God.

Scene 2

Setting: heaven

Props: ornate table with fine china and candles

(Mikey walks in and looks in awe at an ornate banquet table down-stage-right.)

God: Mikey!

Mikey: What?

God: You're here. I'm so glad!

Mikey: Well, I'm sure you're busy. I won't stay long.

God: Why?

Mikey: I'm sure you have better things to do.

God: Why do you say that?

Mikey: Well, you're God and I'm . . . me.

God: That's right. I'm God and you are my beautiful child. Have a seat, Mikey.

Mikey: No, I couldn't.

God: Why not?

Mikey: God, you don't want me sitting at your table.

God: You're the guest of honor! Of course I want you sitting at my table.

Mikey: God, you know me. You know everything about me. I don't deserve a place at your table.

God: Mikey, I don't love you for what you've done. I love you for who you are. Now, accept my acceptance and enjoy the feast.

Mikey: *(sitting)* All this for me?

God: For you and everyone else who will come. Mikey, tell the others. Invite your friends. There's room for everyone.

⊶ ⚌✦⚌ ⊷

*Almighty God, you show the light of your truth
to those in darkness, to lead them into the way of
righteousness. Give strength to all who are joined in the
family of the church, so that they will resolutely reject
what erodes their faith and firmly follow what faith
requires. Through your Son, Jesus Christ, our Lord,
who lives and reigns with you and the Holy Spirit,
one God, now and forever. Amen*

Acts of a
Dying Church

Text: Matthew 28:16-20

Key idea: Sometimes Christians are the church's
worst enemy.

Characters: Elder
                  Secretary
                  Edith Tofflemeyer
                  Barry
                  Brother (Fred) Franklin

Setting: A church sanctuary. The Elder and the
Secretary sit at a table with two microphones.
The rest of the cast sits in the audience with the
congregation.

Props: a karaoke machine; minutes from the last
meeting (for the Secretary)

*Note: The presentation will be funnier if the Elder and the
Secretary act uncomfortable speaking in front of people.*

Elder: I'd like to thank you all for taking the time for
this emergency meeting of First Central Church.
Our pastor, Reverend Johnson, could not make it
this evening due to the restraining order placed upon
him by Brother Carlson. In his absence, I have agreed
to lead tonight's meeting. I think you all know why
we're here. But to comply with Robert's Rules of
Order, the secretary will now read the minutes of the
last annual meeting.

Secretary: Certainly. The meeting was called to order
by the chair, Mr. Anderson, at 7:03 P.M. The treasurer,
Mr. Lewis, reported a 5 percent decline in giving
over the past fiscal year, leaving us unable to pay
the pastoral staff for the month of December.

Mr. Anderson reported a 10 percent decline in
attendance. Discussion ensued as to how to increase
attendance. Edith Tofflemeyer suggested the purchase
of a karaoke machine to liven up our Sunday morning
singing. A motion was passed to purchase said karaoke
machine for a price not to exceed 150 dollars. A
scuffle broke out between Edith Tofflemeyer and the
Robinson boys over the type of music to be played
on the machine. The police arrived at 8 P.M., with
the Robinson boys conceding defeat at 8:05.

Brother Franklin then stood up, and with a very red
face announced , and I quote, "If you people think
I'm going to hang around and let some illegal-alien

karaoke lead our worship, you've got another thing coming." Chairman Anderson then explained that a karaoke was not a person but a machine. Brother Franklin responded, and I quote, "I'm not being mean. I just question God's love for the Karaokes."

The rest of the meeting was spent discussing what to do with the memorial gift provided by the Kern family in the amount of 1,000 dollars. Meredith Reid moved that we spend the money on a new neon cross for the roof. Discussion ensued over whether there were any biblical mandates pertaining to neon crosses. Brother Franklin brought up the "let your light shine bright" passage. The motion was seconded and approved. The meeting was adjourned at 11 P.M.

Elder: Do I hear a motion to accept the minutes as read?

Edith: So moved.

Elder: Do I hear a second?

Secretary: Second.

Elder: All those in favor say "aye."

(All say "aye" except for brother Franklin.)

Elder: Those opposed say nay.

Franklin: Nay.

Elder: Sorry, Brother Franklin, you lose again. Thank you, Mr. Secretary, that was a spirited meeting. On to tonight's business. As you know, we've come to a crucial point in our church's history. With the continued decline in attendance and a mortgage payment that won't go away, we must decide tonight whether we can continue to keep our doors open. I will entertain suggestions from the floor regarding our dilemma.

Barry: Well, the wife and I were talking about it, and we've decided we'd be willing to spearhead a bingo night.

Elder: Hey, now there's an idea. I think everyone in the community enjoys a good game of the old B-I-N-G-O. My concern, of course, would be how much is it going to cost?

Barry: Well, we could have a fund-raiser, perhaps a car wash or something.

Elder: Would you be willing to spearhead the car wash also, Barry?

Barry: Oh, there you go spreading me too thin. There are other people in the church. Let them do the car wash.

Elder: Is there anyone who would like to spearhead the car wash? *(Brother Franklin raises his hand.)* Brother Franklin, would you like to spearhead the car wash?

Franklin: No, I want to talk about this fellow "Krakatoa." Where is he?

Elder: I don't know who you're talking about, Brother Franklin.

Franklin: Yes, you do! "Krakatoa," the worship leader.

Elder: You mean "karaoke"?

Franklin: Whatever! Where is he? We paid this gentleman 150 dollars to lead some singing, and I ain't seen hide nor hair of him.

Elder: Brother Franklin *(pointing to the karaoke machine)*, this is the karaoke machine.

Brother: I'm not being mean. I just want to see the guy!

Elder: Brother Franklin, there is no guy. It's just a machine!

Brother: *(realizing his error)* Oh. Well, that's the most ridiculous thing I've ever seen.

Elder: Back to the car-wash issue . . .

Edith: I think we should have a nice, pretty parade.

Elder: Well, Sister Tofflemeyer, I agree that a parade would be nice. But I don't know . . .

Edith: It will be a statement to the community. We can decorate our cars and hand out balloons.

Franklin: We can bring along "Mr. Krakaroke" there and say, "Look, everyone, we paid 150 bucks for a box that sings! And we even gave it a name—"Krakaroke"!

Elder: Now, Brother Franklin.

Barry: Well, obviously no one here cares about bingo!

Edith: We could create a big float with dandelions.

Secretary: How about an old-fashion hayride? The kids love a hay ride.

Franklin: I'm not going on any hayride with a church that sings to a box.

Elder: Now, Fred.

Jesus: *(offstage voice)* Excuse me. Would someone please explain to me why this church exists?

Elder: *(looking offstage, toward the voice)* Sir, you're new here, aren't you?

Jesus: You could say that.

Elder: What's your name again?

Jesus: Jesus.

Elder: Well, I'm sorry, sir, but you're not a member here, so you don't get to vote.

Almighty God, dwelling in majesty and mystery, renewing and fulfilling creation by your eternal Spirit, and revealing your glory through our Lord, Jesus Christ. Cleanse us from doubt and fear, and enable us to worship you, with your Son and the Holy Spirit, one God, living and reigning, now and forever. Amen

Blind Spots

Text: Romans 3:19-28

Key idea: Christianity is a relationship more than a religion.

Characters: Dr. Sawyer
  Ms. Johnson

Setting: an optometrist's office

Props: Eyeglasses. Bible. If a projector is available, the following slides can be used as eye charts:

Eye chart #1: R-U-L-E-S

  A-B-S-U-R-D

  N-A-R-R-O-W-M-I-N-D-E-D

Eye chart #2: C-H-R-I-S-T-I-A-N-I-T-Y

  J-E-S-U-S-C-H-R-I-S-T

(Johnson sits in the office as Sawyer enters.)

Sawyer: Hello there, I'm Dr. Sawyer. You must be Ms. Johnson.

Johnson: Yes. It's a pleasure to meet you.

Sawyer: Likewise. What seems to be the problem?

Johnson: Well, I'm having trouble seeing certain things.

Sawyer: I see. Do me a favor. Do you see that chart on the wall? *(Displays chart #1)* Read the first line please.

Johnson: C-H-R-I-S-T-I-A-N-I-T-Y . . . Christianity.

Sawyer: Good. Now the next line.

Johnson: R-U-L-E-S . . . Rules.

Sawyer: Interesting. Try the next line.

Johnson: A-B-S-U-R-D . . . Absurd.

Sawyer: Fascinating. Now try one more line.

Johnson: N-A-R-R-O-W-M-I-N-D-E-D . . . Narrow-minded.

Sawyer: Let me ask you something. How long have you been wearing glasses?

Johnson: Since childhood.

Sawyer: Did you go to church as a child?

Johnson: What does this have to do with . . .

Sawyer: Just trust me.

Johnson: Yes, I did.

Sawyer: What do you remember about it?

Johnson: I remember the pastor yelling a lot about how we break all the rules.

Sawyer: When did you stop going to church?

Johnson: How did you know? . . . Well, let's see, I guess when I was in college.

Sawyer: Why did you drop out?

Johnson: The whole thing just seemed absurd, and everyone involved in it seemed so narrow-minded.

Sawyer: I want you to do something for me. Take off your glasses and try reading this. *(Hands Johnson a Bible)* Read that verse.

Johnson: Matthew 5:43-44. "You have heard that it was said, 'You shall love your neighbor and hate your enemy.' But I say to you, Love your enemies and pray for those who persecute you."

Sawyer: Does that sound narrow-minded to you?

Johnson: No, I guess not.

Sawyer: How about this one?

Johnson: Matthew 11:28: "Come to me, all you that are weary and carrying burdens, and I will give you rest."

Sawyer: Does that sound absurd to you?

Johnson: No.

Sawyer: How about this one?

Johnson: Matthew 22:37-40. "You shall love the Lord your God with all your heart, and with all your soul, and with all your mind.' This is the greatest and first commandment. And the second is like it: 'You shall love your neighbor as yourself.' On these two commandments hang all the law and the prophets."

Sawyer: Does that sound like just a bunch of rules and regulations?

Johnson: Who said all this stuff?

Sawyer: Jesus Christ. Now, would you mind reading the chart again?

(Johnson displays chart #2)

Johnson: C-H-R-I-S-T-I-A-N-I-T-Y. Christianity.

Sawyer: Good. Now the next line.

Johnson: J-E-S-U-S-C-H-R-I-S-T, Jesus Christ.

Sawyer: There you go. Now, I'm going to write you out a prescription here. Take this to any bookstore and buy a B-I-B-L-E . . . Bible. I believe it will help you see the Savior a bit better.

Johnson: *(referring to glasses)* What should I do with these?

Sawyer: Give them to me. I'll burn them. Glasses like these cause eternal damage.

Almighty God, pour out your Holy Spirit upon your faithful people. Keep them steadfast in your Word, protect and comfort them in all temptations, defend them against all their enemies, and bestow on the church your saving peace. Through your Son, Jesus Christ, our Lord, who lives and reigns with you and the Holy Spirit, one God, now and forever. Amen

Appendix

Pages 78-80 list the dramas in the order they appear in this book, along with their key ideas, related lectionary texts, and a suggested presentation day for each sketch.

Drama Title	Key Idea	Lectionary Text	Church Day/Year
God's Walking Gift p. 18	"God with us" means that God knows and loves us.	Matthew 1: 18-25 (v. 23)	Fourth Sunday in Advent, year A
The Shepherd p. 23	Jesus' birth did not bring complete safety to the world.	Luke 1:39-55 (vv. 46-55)	Fourth Sunday in Advent, year C
Crisscrossed Christmas p. 26	Christmas traditions go many directions. Only one is toward Christ.	Titus 3:4-7	The Nativity of Our Lord, years A, B, C
Walter the Whiner p. 33	Integrating Christianity into the fabric of life.	Colossians 3: 12-17	First Sunday after Christmas, year C
Peculiar Petitions p. 37	Prayer is more than a formula with easy answers.	Matthew 4:5-13	Fourth Sunday after the Epiphany, year B

Drama Title	Key Idea	Lectionary Text	Church Day/Year
Common Ground p. 42	Freedom in Christ.	1 Corinthians 8: 1-13 (vv. 1-8)	Fourth Sunday after the Epiphany, year B
Ladder-Climbing p. 47	Distracted from God by work, selfishness, pride, and success.	1 Corinthians 3: 10-11, 16-23	Seventh Sunday after the Epiphany, Proper 2, year A
Weak-Kneed Wishes p. 52	Radical faith brings a radical response.	Mark 2:1-12	Seventh Sunday after the Epiphany, Proper 2, year B
Wah! Wah! Wah! p. 55	Worrying is an excuse to avoid real life.	Matthew 6: 25-34	Eighth Sunday after the Epiphany, Proper 3, year A
The Church of Dr. Shaman Guru p. 59	Must it be a physical resurrection?	John 20:24-29	Second Sunday of Easter, years A, B, C
Invitation p. 63	God's invitation to the feast boosts our passion for life.	Psalm 23 (vv. 5-6)	Fourth Sunday of Easter, years A, B, C

Drama Title	Key Idea	Lectionary Text	Church Day/Year
Acts of a Dying Church p. 68	Sometimes Christians are the church's worst enemy.	Matthew 28: 16-20	Holy Trinity, year A
Blind Spots p. 74	Christianity is a relationship more than a religion.	Romans 3:19-28	Reformation Day, years A, B, C